WELCOME HOME

A Little Book of
Greeting and Thanksgiving

SPRING SUNSHINE, OAKWOOD, SURREY   H. Smith

It was for their sakes you endured the long years,
and they know! They waited too . . .

From Haven Green Church, Ealing, to those of its fellowship who served in the King's Forces during the World War, 1939-45, in much gratitude and with good wishes for the Peace so hardly and so triumphantly won.

Presented at
Welcome Home Social Gathering.
Wednesday, June 5th, 1946.

J. MacBeath
.... Minister.

WELCOME HOME

A Little Book
of Greeting and Thanksgiving

LESLIE F. CHURCH
B.A., Ph.D.

THE EPWORTH PRESS
(EDGAR C. BARTON)
25-35 City Road, London, E.C.1

CONTENTS

I
Welcome

A hundred thousand welcomes: I could weep,
And I could laugh; I am light and heavy—
*   welcome!*

SHAKESPEARE

THIS little book is written because *you* are coming home and someone is very glad—and thankful. There is no single word which could tell you how glad they are, but ' welcome ', at any rate, suggests a kind reception. The dictionary says that it originally referred to ' a comer for another's pleasure '. Well, you are all that—and much more. They are proud of your service, and perhaps will find it hard to say so in words, but they have missed you through the long months and years. Life has not been easy without you, but they have tried to carry on, and when you get back you will find they have kept your seat !

You have missed them, too. How often I have heard you talk, in far-off places, of home and the people there. In Friendship House at Baghdad, and in that lonely tent at El Alamein you did not ask me for arguments, but for news of folk at home. It was the same in the grim unhappiness of Nisida and the unreality of Rome. By runways and on troopships, in the wards at Bari and El Balah, in the desolate wastes round Terhag, at Geneifa and Kassassin, in Damascus, and on the Shepherds' Fields at Bethlehem that starlit night—you did not ask for lectures on antiquities but, first, you asked for word of those you left at home. It was for their sakes you endured the long years, and they know! They waited too, and now they give you eager welcome. The joy of your return is almost pain.

You have set the peoples free, and now your own time of liberation has come. I think I know how you feel—a little anxious and not quite sure of yourself. The years have changed so many things that you almost shrink from that first meeting, and the future is uncertain.

First of all we want you to know you are welcome for your own sake, whether you come from Burma or Paiforce, from M.E.F. or C.M.F. or B.L.A. or anywhere on the Seven Seas. Then we want to face the problem of beginning again and going on— together. That is why we offer you this little book—and remember, someone who has been thinking and praying for you has sent it. Again 'a hundred thousand welcomes', and God bless your home-coming.

ON THE WAY HOME

HUMANITY in its ascent to the Father returns homewards, not as it left, but with all the gathered wealth of experience. It has sounded the depths, and learned humility in sinfulness, gained strength through its utter weakness, and been made perfect through suffering.

Anonymous

RESTORED! Returned! The lost are borne
On seas of shipwreck home at last:
See! In the fire of praising burns
The dry dumb past, and we
The life-day long shall part no more.

W. H. Auden

HOWEVER long and rough the road it's easier walking if a man knows that round the last bend he'll see the lights of home.

Leslie F. Church

BUT to come home at evening down the slack,
And see the kindly smoke curl from the stack!

But to come home at dark, and see again
Welcoming firelight on the window-pane!

But to come home, come home; and find once
    more
An open door!

Wilfrid Gibson

SPRINGTIME in England!
And the green leaves show
God's little heralds in the green hedgerow,
And the golden daffodils
And the pale hyacinths
And the young, lusty winds in the elms!

Springtime in England!
There's frolic in the dales,
While the ewe lambs dance and the shepherd
    tells his tales,
And the patient shepherd dog,
And the busy browsing sheep
And the cool, playful winds in the elms.

Springtime in England!
Where the pure air chastens;
Cool Sabbath evenings when the twilight
    hastens;
And the distant chapel bell,
And the silent village street,
And the rustling of the wind in the elms.

Springtime in England! Diamonds in the sun
Tiny drops each choosing its couch to lie upon;
And the tiny, trembling daisy
And the four-leaved clover
And the gentle, soothing wind in the elms.

For it's Springtime in England
And for one who's far away,
There's a dreadful, hungry yearning
For the coming of 'the day':
To see the village street,
To hear the chapel bell,
And the sighing, longing wind in the elms.

> A. R. Annakin—Lines written in South
> Tunisia, March 1943. The writer
> was killed in action 6th April 1943

London—from Westminster Bridge

EARTH has not anything to show more fair:
Dull would he be of soul who could pass by
A sight so touching in its majesty:
This City now doth, like a garment, wear
The beauty of the morning; silent, bare,
Ships, towers, domes, theatres and temples lie
Open unto the fields, and to the sky;
All bright and glittering in the smokeless air.
Never did sun more beautifully steep
In his first splendour, valley, rock, or hill;
Ne'er saw I, never felt, a calm so deep!
The river glideth at his own sweet will:
Dear God! the very houses seem asleep;
And all that mighty heart is lying still!

> William Wordsworth

ONE man with a dream, at pleasure,
Shall go forth and conquer a crown . . .

THEY knew that life brought its contest, but they expected from it also the crown of all contest. No proud one! no jewelled circlet flaming through Heaven above the height of the unmerited throne; only some few leaves of wild olive, cool to the tired brow, through a few years of peace. . . . Not in war, not in wealth, not in tyranny, was there any happiness to be found for them—only in kindly peace, fruitful and free. The wreath was to be of wild olive, mark you—the tree that grows carelessly, tufting the rocks with no vivid bloom, no verdure of branch, only with soft snow of blossoms and scarcely fulfilled fruit, mixed with grey leaf and thorn-set stem. . . . But this, such as it is, you may win, while yet you live; type of grey honour and sweet rest. Freeheartedness, and graciousness, and undisturbed trust, and requited love, and the sight of the peace of others, and the ministry of their pain —these, and the blue sky above you, and the sweet waters and flowers of the earth beneath; and mysteries and presences innumerable of living things, may yet be here your riches; untormenting and divine; serviceable for the life that now is; nor, it may be, without promise of that which is to come.

John Ruskin

BE thou faithful unto death, and I will give thee a crown of life.

Rev. ii. 10

II
Home

SUTTON POYNTZ, DORSET   *H. A. Summers*

You are coming back to the land you have served so
well, to its mountains, its rivers, and its plains, to the
towns and villages you lived in . . . but the heart of
all your memories is home.

II

Home

You are coming back—to the land you have served so well, to its mountains, its rivers and its plains, to the towns and villages you lived in, perhaps to the job you had before you went away. All these places you have remembered many a time, but the heart of all your memories is home. There you grew up, or there your children are growing up now, or maybe it is still the pattern in a dream that you are going to make reality.

When you wrote from the 'forward areas' you often said to yourself, 'I won't write about this or that; I don't want to scare them at home'. That was because you cared. Someone in the B.L.A. said not long ago, 'I think the soldier's real concern is not the war, not politics, not the future of the world, but his family'. He spoke as a young soldier on active service in a dangerous spot. It was because you cared so much that you fought so well. Millions of homes are safe, and millions more will come into being because men like you did not tire in the great crusade.

And yet it is not easy to come home! You have been away so long. A little child of three, who had never seen her father, heard he was coming back. The mother tried to prepare her for the great event. She looked puzzled, and then said : 'But Mummy, do I shake hands with him or can I kiss him?' I have not forgotten the look on the mother's face as she told me. . . . The old intimacies seem strange when it is years since they found full expression, but do not get the idea that they are gone for ever. You who have learned to know the fundamental values in the hardships of campaigning should know what really endures in spite of every separation. Love never fails, but love is also 'very patient'. It will take more than a moment to get right back home! The settling down and the readjustments will take time. *You* will need it, and so will those to whom you are coming. They have changed and so have you, but if the love that binds you has not changed, you need not be afraid. It will work out the differences. The tragedy of war, with all its sacrifices of precious years, need not have wrecked your personal relationships. You are coming home, and there you may learn that the long years of serving and of waiting have only strengthened the bonds that bind you into one family. Faith in God, who is Love, will help you to win that final victory.

LAND OF HEART'S DESIRE

GREEN fields of England! whereso'er
Across this watery waste we fare,
One image at our hearts we bear,
Green fields of England, everywhere.

Sweet eyes in England, I must flee
Past where the waves' last confines be
Ere your loved smile I cease to see,
Sweet eyes in England, dear to me.

Dear home in England, safe and fast,
If but in thee my lot be cast,
The past shall seem a nothing past
To thee, dear home, if won at last;
Dear home in England, won at last.

Arthur Hugh Clough

THE man of high descent may love the halls
and lands of his inheritance as a part of himself, as trophies of his birth and power; the
poor man's attachment to the tenement he
holds, which strangers have held before, and
may tomorrow occupy again, has a worthier
root, struck deep into purer soil. His household
gods are of flesh and blood, with no alloy of
silver, gold, or precious stones; he has no
property but in the affectations of his own
heart; and when they endear bare floors and
walls, despite of toil and scanty meals, that
man has his love of home from God, and his
rude hut becomes a solemn place. **Dickens**

A Wife

SHE had within her being a Holy of Holies where she sat alone and where the presence of her dearest was forbidden. In the long, dark nights of the Lossiemouth late autumn and winter, with the moan of the sea passing over the land like the cry of toiling creation, the call of the night bird flying overhead, and the mass of stars shining above her, she would retire within herself and go out silently to the shore or the moors in quest of something which haunts life like a dim vision of a strange beauty or a confused echo of a far-away melody.

Ramsay Macdonald

A Mother

IN her happiest moments—and never was a happier woman—her mouth did not of a sudden begin to twitch, and tears to lie on the mute blue eyes in which I have read all I know and would ever care to write. For when you looked into my mother's eyes you knew, as if He had told you, why God sent her into the world—it was to open the minds of all who look to beautiful thoughts.

James Barrie

A Home

I CANNOT but marvel at the skill that secured its comfort for all of us. A happier household, I believe, there never was; and though my father, I should say, never made a pound a week, we never lacked anything, so far as I could see, whether in the way of wholesome food or of comfortable and respectable clothing. Of course it is not possible to make the 'plenty' of a good working-man's home intelligible to the well-to-do. Things which look like impossibilities are achieved every day; and the so-called Laws of Domestic Economy are abstract generalities compared with the concrete sense and skill of the clever mother. Let me illustrate. Seven persons had all their meals every day in that little ten-foot kitchen, where the food was cooked and the family lived. There was no room for all to sit at our table; neither the table nor the room was big enough. What then? The answer is simple; we took our meals in relays. First came my two elder brothers, both of them apprentice gardeners at the squire's. . . . My brothers generally arrived home at midday ravenously hungry. . . . After them came father, bringing his princely good-nature and unselfishness and splendid appetite; and with him came one (or sometimes two) of his workmen. What meal I had I generally took standing, being always in a hurry to go out to play. When my youngest sister fed I cannot remember; but everything that concerned her was 'special'. My mother sat at peace to her dinner later on, after she had attended to all our meals, and she ate it at leisure.

Let me give another example. There was no room for the cradle in the day-time on that crowded ten-foot floor, when my second, little, short-lived sister was born. What was to be done? Well! the cradle was put upstairs, a string was let down from it through a hole in the low ceiling, and whenever the baby cried my mother bade one of us pull the string. I can hear the rick-rock of the cradle above my head even yet, when I sit down to listen to old memories. . . .

No indignity was meant; none was ever thought of. We were all partners in one family enterprise, and all things ran smoothly in their course. . . . But we helped, and I think I may say, we inspired each other; and we were very happy.

A better-fitted pair than my father and mother there could hardly be. She ruled always in little things, and my father's attitude to her was obviously idolatrous, and charming to witness. Hers to him was mischievous to the last degree, and his patience occasionally gave way for brief moments. Then he would grumble, and endure and join in the fun.

> Sir Henry Jones, C.H. (Professor of Moral Philosophy in the University of Glasgow)

WHAT joy is like it? to be quit of care
And drop my load, and after weary miles
Come home, and sink upon the bed that so
I used to dream of: this one thing is worth
All that long service. Hail, sweet Sirmio!
Welcome thy lord with laughter, and give back
Your laughter, waters of the Lydian lake:
Laugh, home of mine, with all your maddest
     mirth. Catullus

A MAN'S HOME

HOME—the nursery of the infinite.

Channing

HOME is the residence not merely of the body but of the heart . . .

Anonymous

HOME that our feet may leave but not our hearts.

O. W. Holmes

MY idea of a home is a house in which each member of the family can on the instant kindle a fire in his or her private room.

Ralph Waldo Emerson

A HOUSE full of books and a garden of flowers.

Andrew Lang

ONLY a man harrowing clods
  In a slow silent walk
With an old horse that stumbles and nods
  Half asleep as they stalk.

Only thin smoke without flame
  From the heaps of couch grass;
Yet this will go onward the same
  Though Dynasties pass.

Yonder a maid and her wight
  Come whispering by:
War's annals will cloud into night
  Ere their story die.

Thomas Hardy

SUCH is the patriot's boast, where'er we roam
His first, best country ever is, at home.

Oliver Goldsmith

TELL me, gentle traveller, who hast wandered
through the world, and seen the sweetest roses
blow, and brightest gliding rivers—of all thine
eyes have seen, which is the fairest land?

' Child shall I tell thee where Nature is most
blest and fair? It is where those we love abide.
Though that space be small, ample is it above
kingdoms; though it be a desert, through it
runs the river of Paradise, and there are the
enchanted bowers.'

Ibn Ahmed Attar

SURELY there is nought sweeter than a man's
own country and his parents, even though he
dwell far off in a rich home, in a strange land,
away from them that begat him.

Homer

IT's a corner of heaven itself,
    Though it's only a tumble-down nest,
But with love brooding there, why, no place
    can compare
    With my little grey home in the west.

D. Eardley Wilmot

III

The Years of Absence :
Wasted Years ?

BALLINTOY COTTAGES, IRELAND   *Fox Photos Ltd.*

But with love brooding there, why, no place can
     compare
With my little grey home in the west. . . .

III

The Years of Absence : Wasted Years?

ONE day in Syria a sapper showed me a photograph of himself before he joined up. I saw the picture of a young man with a youthful face. When he gave it to me he said, 'Look at that. That's what I was four years ago. Look at me now—nearly bald-headed, face lined like a railway track, just a perishing old man.' It was partly true—all but the last phrase. He had certainly aged and the East had taken its toll of him. He waited eagerly for what I had to say. 'Do you know what *she* did this morning?' I asked. 'She stood before her mirror, doing her hair, and frowned as she looked at her picture in the glass. There were a few wrinkles, and even a grey hair or two. She snapped at the scowling face reflected there. "Wonder if he'll care for that!" she said. She isn't the girl you left behind, old man. She's something much more wonderful. She's a woman who's come through the fires of war, and—she's waiting for her man. She's not expecting a playboy to come back.' He coughed a little in embarrassment, turned on his heel to go away but, as he went, he smiled. 'Maybe you're right, padre,' he said.

I knew I was right—but the mirror had not lied. She is no longer a girl, nor even a woman without knowledge. She, too, has looked death in the face. Yes, they have both changed. The years of separation and hardship have left their mark on them, but were they wasted years? Is it all to be written off as dead loss?

The pessimist looks back and cries with W. B. Yeats :

The years like great black oxen tread the world,
And God the herdsman goads them on behind,
And I am broken by their passing feet.

The optimist looking toward the future reckons his gains in comradeship, in experience, and in character. With a new sense of eternal values he shouts defiance at the years. They cannot storm the inner citadel of his invincible spirit any more than the mirror or the camera can picture the soul!

'Be not afraid of life.' As you come home, thank God that you have tried to do your duty and accept the new adventure that awaits you. It is said that Henry IV of France reproved Crillon because he was late at the battle of Arques. 'Go away and hang yourself, Crillon,' he said. 'We fought at

Arques and you were not there.' When the
fate of humanity hung in the balance, when
Evil with tremendous armies attacked the
liberties of man, you *were* there. However
small you knew yourself to be—you were
there. The enemy was turned to flight. All
the dismal prophets were confounded. The
battle was won against insuperable odds—
and *you* were there. No man, nor even Father
Time, can rob you of that recorded fact.
You will not strut like an arrogant bully,
shouting that you did a great deed by yourself! You know that, somehow, you were
upheld.

There were moments when mathematics
declared the day was lost. There were
moments when common sense said the only
thing left was to surrender. It seemed
impossible that you, as an individual, could
survive. Yet the day was won, the surrender
was never made and you are coming home.
As a great Air-Marshal said of the Battle of
Britain : ' There were evidences that pointed
to divine intervention which those in high
command came to recognize, and through
which they felt that they were watching
part of God's plan of the ages working out.'

Your experience of these years may be the
basis for a triumphant faith—a faith which
can conquer the very things you dread, the
future, old age, the career broken by long

19

service overseas. The years like great black oxen do tread the world, but you need not be broken. 'He hath delivered you from the horns of the wild oxen.'

Be like Admiral Nimitz—'a man of cheerful yesterdays and confident tomorrows'. Those years of separation were not all loss. Think on their gains and face the future unafraid.

. . . . .

There are some who will come back with memories that hurt—memories of their own folly. There are some who set out to wait faithfully at home, but were not true. What of the home-coming then? For such there is but one place of beginning again. It is at the mercy-seat of God. There the penitent may find pardon and peace and the gift of patience which will suffice even for that long trek back.

. . . . .

The prophet, speaking for God Himself, gave us a promise that still holds good: 'I will restore the years the locust hath eaten.' The poet, challenging his pessimistic brothers, calls us to climb the heights:

Nor deem the irrevocable Past
    As wholly wasted, wholly vain,
If, rising on its wrecks, at last
    To something nobler we attain.

20

We will not look back but forward, not down
but up. On then—to build the City of God.

COMRADES OF THE STORM

WHATEVER the years have taken, they have
given you a comradeship which shall endure.
To share hardship, to struggle side by side
against great odds, to look death in the face
and, above all, to talk together, sometimes, of
the Tomorrow you risked your lives to win—
these are the things which bind you in a fellowship that must not pass away.

Leslie F. Church

Eve of Agincourt

HE that outlives this day, and comes safe home,
Will stand a tiptoe when this day is nam'd.

.   .   .   .   .

He that shall live this day, and see old age,
Will yearly on the vigil feast his neighbours,
And say, 'Tomorrow is Saint Crispian':
Then will he strip his sleeves and show his scars,
And say, 'These wounds I had on Crispin's
    day.'
And Crispin Crispian shall ne'er go by,
From this day to the ending of the world,
But we in it shall be remembered;
We few, we happy few, we band of brothers;
For he today that sheds his blood with me
Shall be my brother; be he ne'er so vile
This day shall gentle his condition.

Shakespeare

FAITH IN THE FUTURE

John Bright Speaks Out

Is this a reality? Or is your Christianity a romance? Is your profession a dream? No, I am sure that your Christianity is not a romance; your profession is not a dream. It is because I believe this that I appeal to you with confidence, and that I have hope and faith in the future. I believe that we shall see, and at no very distant time, sound economic principles spreading much more widely among the people; a sense of justice growing up in soil which hitherto has been deemed unfruitful and, which will be better than all, the churches of Great Britain awaking as it were from their slumbers, and girding up their loins to more glorious work, when they shall not only accept and believe in the prophecy but labour earnestly for its fulfilment, that there shall come a time, a blessed time, a time which shall last for ever, when nation shall not lift up sword against nation, neither shall they learn war any more.

John Bright

EVER the faith endures,
  England, my England:
'Take and break us: we are yours,
  England, my own!
Life is good, and joy runs high
Between English earth and sky;
Death is death; but we shall die
  To the song on your bugles blown, England.'

W. E. Henley

So . . . I feel in regard to this aged England
. . . pressed upon by transitions of trade and
. . . competing populations,—I see her not
dispirited, not weak, but well remembering that
she has seen dark days before;—indeed, with a
kind of instinct that she sees a little better on
a cloudy day, and that, in storm of battle and
calamity, she has a secret vigour and a pulse
like a cannon.

Ralph Waldo Emerson

To the boy at the high room window,
   Gazing alone and apart,
There came a wish without reason,
   A thought that shone through his heart.
' I will take this moment and keep it ',
   He said to himself, ' for a vow,
To remember for ever and ever,
   As if it were always now.'

Laurence Binyon

Follow with reverent steps the great example
   Of Him whose holy work was doing good;
So shall the wide earth seem our Father's
   temple,
   Each loving life a psalm of gratitude.

Then shall all shackles fall; the stormy
   clangour
   Of wild war-music o'er the earth shall cease;
Love shall tread out the baleful fires of anger,
   And in its ashes plant the tree of peace.

John Greenleaf Whittier

HIGH RESOLVE

. . . . WE here highly resolve that the dead shall not have died in vain, that this nation, under God, shall have a new birth of freedom. . . .

Abraham Lincoln

Ulysses Sails On

It may be we shall touch the Happy Isles,
And see the great Achilles, whom we knew,
Though much is taken, much abides; and though
We are not now that strength which in old days
Moved earth and heaven; that which we are
    we are:
One equal temper of heroic hearts,
Made weak by time and fate, but strong in will
To strive, to seek, to find, and not to yield.

Tennyson

'WOULD'ST thou'—so the helmsman
        answered,—
    'Learn the secret of the sea?
Only those who brave its dangers
    Comprehend its mystery!'

Longfellow

I dream'd in a dream I saw a city invincible to
    the attacks of the whole of the rest of
    the earth,
I dream'd that was the new city of Friends.

Walt Whitman

IV

Was it Worth While ?

SAILOR'S BOYS   *H. A. Summers*

You shall find the reward of your sacrifices, your
loneliness, and your long years of absence, in the quiet
homes, the smiling children . . .

IV

Was it Worth While?

EVERY service man reserves the right to grouse. It is often the result of a mood or some passing circumstance rather than a considered conviction. All the same, he has seen so many things that deserved criticism that he comes back sometimes wondering whether he need have gone at all. As a modern humorist has put it, 'if not actually disgruntled, he is far from being gruntled!'

We are not the first people to ask ourselves whether a nation's sacrifice was worth while. It was William Pitt who answered the question for us when he said, long ago, 'What we have gained by the war is, in one word, all that we should have lost without it'. We who are so weary of propaganda that we are inclined to mistrust too much need not go to books or speeches for the list of things we know were threatened with destruction—precious things which remain for us and for our children and, when they have learned their supreme value, for all humanity. Freedom has not perished!

When the Allied Military currency was

printed for use in Italy the Four Freedoms were stamped upon the back of every note. Even a single lire, worth less than a penny, bore the words: Freedom of Speech, Freedom of Religion, Freedom from Want, and Freedom from Fear. These things remain and you helped to preserve them, because in your heart you believed in that greater freedom which makes a man free enough to bind himself to the best he knows.

Was it worth while? Look where you will you shall find the reward of your sacrifices, your loneliness and your long years of absence, in the quiet homes, the smiling children, the fields moving silently to abundant harvest, the men and women busied in honourable toil and the old folk shaping their closing years in the noble pattern of a prayer.

When people asked Dr. Schweitzer why, in burying himself in the heart of Africa to build a hospital, he made so great a sacrifice, he answered: ' There is no such thing as sacrifice if the cause be big enough.' You gave the precious years to help to stamp out an intolerable evil and to lay the foundations of new happiness for all the world. That was worth while.

SOME THINGS YOU SAVED

MANY of England's ancient monuments are damaged or gone for ever. The blitz has passed over cities, ports, churches, temples, humble homes and palaces, Houses of Parliament and Law Courts. Irreplaceable treasures of a thousand years of almost uninterrupted progress and culture and peaceful civilization have disappeared for ever. Much is gone which is lost for ever.

But one thing is not lost—one thing, the most precious of all, remains and has rather increased. For what will it profit a nation if it wins the whole world and loses its soul? The soul remains, glory has not departed from the land. I speak not of outward glory, of what your Gallic neighbours call 'la Gloire'. I speak rather of that inward glory, that splendour of the spirit, which has shone over this land from the soul of its people, and has been a beacon light to the oppressed and down-trodden people in this new martyrdom of man.

General Smuts, 1942

To re-quote a great Prime Minister you have so lived and given of your best that your children will feel the joy you felt of primroses in spring, the scent of morning meadows, the carolling of birds, the good fellowship of market day, the laughter of your children no longer afraid. These things you have preserved for them. It was worth while.

Based on phrases used by William Pitt in 1803

REJOICE, whatever anguish rend your heart,
  That God has given you, for a priceless
    dower,
To live in these great times and have your part
  In Freedom's crowning hour.
That you may tell your sons who see the light
  High in the heaven, their heritage to take :—
  ' I saw the powers of darkness put to flight !
  I saw the morning break ! '

Sir Owen Seaman

WE cannot assume that great nations will at
once become pure altruists or that they will
always be perfectly just to smaller states. But
if they safeguard as Britain has done, the result,
while falling short of Utopia, will be one that
every state should welcome.

Harold Callender

THROUGH all the centuries, and over all
these Southern waters, nameless men have
fought in nameless places, their sole monument
a protected coast and an unravaged countryside.

Conan Doyle

NOT a day passes over the earth, but men and
women of no note do great deeds, speak great
words, and suffer noble sorrows. Of these
obscure heroes, philosophers and martyrs, the
greater part will never be known till that hour
when many that are great be small and the
small great.

Charles Reade

TRUE VALUES

ENGLAND is now learning again that neither wealth nor power nor comfort, whether for class or individual, are ends in themselves : that the wealth of a nation consists in nothing but the virtue of her children and children's children. That no profits, education, law, custom, or institution that does not contribute to their health and goodness is of any enduring value. That the proper test of all legislation, of every political programme and economic activity, is not 'Does it pay?' or 'Does it enrich this class or that?' but 'Will it make better men and women?'

An island fortress, England has fought a war of redemption not only for Europe but for her own soul. Facing dangers greater than any in her history, she has fallen back on the rock of her natural character. Her future and that of the world depend not only on her victory but on her ability to restate in a new form the ancient laws of her own moral purpose and unity. By so doing she may discover a common denominator for human reconstruction more glorious than anything in her long past.

Arthur Bryant

THE fact is made plainer than it ever was before that English-speaking men are friends and friends for the largest purpose of civilization.

Walter Hines Page

Columbus Speaks to God

ALL my emprises have been filled with Thee,
My speculations, plans, begun and carried on in
thoughts of Thee;
Sailing the deep or journeying the land for
Thee;
Intentions, purports, aspirations mine, leaving
results to Thee.

O I am sure they really came from Thee,
The urge, the ardour, the unconquerable will,
The potent, felt, interior command, stronger
than words,
A message from the heavens, whispering to me
even in sleep,
These sped me on.

The end I know not, it is all in Thee,
Or small or great I know not—haply what
broad fields, what lands,
Haply the brutish measureless human under-
growth I know,
Transplanted there may rise to stature, knowledge worthy Thee,
Haply the swords I know may there indeed be
turned to reaping-tools,
Haply the lifeless cross I know, Europe's dead
cross, may bud and blossom there.

Walt Whitman

IT IS NOT FINISHED!

It is surely better for religion to conquer civilization than to destroy it, to harness the brave and brilliant modern energies for the glory of God instead of in the name of God decrying and depressing them. Can we do this? It is our special task at this stage of history. The future will judge us by the extent to which we prove ourselves big and strong enough to take into our grasp the wide and wonderful content of the modern world and unify, purify, fructify it for genuine progress by subduing it all to an adequate vision of God and man.

In the post-war years millions of tortured spirits, and eyes blackened by the sight for years of scarcely anything but evil in its foulest forms, will need a message to cleanse their hearts and widen their outlook and give them a motive to recover faith in man. Only the Church can give it. The Church means you and me, and God. God will do His part. Shall we do ours? Only if, besides declaring the message to be true, we live as though it were. If Christians lose their heads in this greatest of all trials of mankind, they will expose to ridicule not only themselves but also the whole religious view of man.

Prof. T. E. Jessop

MAN isn't man until he is self-transcendent, until he lives for ends, for goals, for ideals which stretch out beyond the world of space and time.

Rufus Jones

For I dipt into the future, far as human eye
    could see,
Saw the Vision of the world, and all the wonder
    that would be;

Saw the heavens fill with commerce, argosies of
    magic sails,
Pilots of the purple twilight, dropping down
    with costly bales;

Heard the heavens fill with shouting, and there
    rain'd a ghastly dew
From the nations' airy navies grappling in the
    central blue;

Far along the world-wide whisper of the South-
    wind rushing warm,
With the standards of the peoples plunging thro'
    the thunderstorm;

Till the war-drums throbb'd no longer, and the
    battle flags were furl'd
In the Parliament of man, the Federation of
    the world.

Tennyson

V

What Now ?

BANGOR AND THE MOUNTAINS OF WALES   *Fox Photos Ltd.*

The mountains also shall bring peace; and the little
hills righteousness unto the people.

V

What Now ?

WILL you be disappointed when you come home? It depends on what you expect to find. Victory in the field is not the end of the task. How many times you have said that the winning of the peace would be harder than the winning of the war. Sometimes you were tempted to say it cynically as though you were to become a mere spectator soon.

In an article written by an officer of the B.L.A. there was this passage: 'It is, perhaps, encouraging that Tommy, 1944, will not be foozled by facile talk of a land fit for heroes. He wants deeds, not words. It is up to the citizens of England to see he is not disappointed.'—But he *is* a citizen! To be demobilized does not deprive him of his citizenship nor relieve him of his responsibility. War-weariness may make him inclined, for a time, to become a cynic, but it does not mean that he leaves the army, as someone has suggested, 'believing in nothing, hoping for nothing, proposing to do nothing about it'.

You have won the victory; you, of all people, must help to consolidate the gains. It was a battle, not for a nation, but for all people everywhere. You have an obligation and an opportunity to shape the future.

Men of vision and men of faith must build not only houses but homes. In a new fellowship of service, and in humble dependence on Almighty God, we may overcome all obstacles, animate and inanimate.

When General Eisenhower ended his memorable speech at the Guildhall, London, he said : ' No petty differences in the world of trade, traditions, or national pride should ever blind us to identities in priceless values. If we keep our eyes on this guide-post then no difficulties along our path of mutual co-operation can ever be insurmountable. Moreover, when this truth has permeated to the remotest hamlet and heart of all peoples, then indeed may we beat our swords into ploughshares, and all nations can enjoy the fruitfulness of the earth.'

These words may be applied not only to nations but to individuals. It is the spiritual values which are the priceless values, and they depend on spiritual relationships between man and man, and between man and God. When these are right, all else will be right. Atomic bombs will be grotesque, and atomic energy will be used to build and not to destroy. The problem of tomorrow's world is, first of all, a problem of spiritual relationships.

MAKING DEMOCRACY SAFE

DEMOCRACY is *not* ripe for destruction, but it is awaiting its deliverance and completion. And these can only take place first, as it returns to its Divine base. . . . It is idle to discuss the future of democracy apart from the religion (i.e. Christianity) which gave birth to it, and which remains its only *raison d'être*. . . . Second, democracy must return to a Christian education for life, beginning with children. . . . By a Christian education is meant teaching of the great truths of the Gospel in their relation to our lives. A Christian education is education for *complete* living as human beings. Third, democracy will find it necessary to readjust itself to entirely new situations. . . . The democratic idea is based upon the truth of man's relation to God as child, and to his fellows as brother. Humanity is one family and it can never be at peace and free to work out its destiny until the family idea returns to us, is freely accepted by us, and life is modelled upon it.

There are sufficient people in the world who believe in the Christian ethic (although they may not accept the Christian faith), and also, if they would agree to unite their forces and, as democrats, would join the Christian army, drilled and fit, could make it desperately difficult, if not impossible, for the anti-Christian and anti-human forces to control the world.

They could not take theft out of the heart of the gangsters, but they could police the Jericho road and protect decent travellers from the robbers. And maybe the robbers would think better of things, and turn to an honest life.

F. C. Spurr

IF you ask me what is wrong with Europe, I should say the moral basis. The bedrock of the Christian moral code has become undermined . . . and the vast whole is now sagging.

Gen. Smuts

IT may well be that the most glorious chapters of our history are yet to be written. Indeed the very problems and dangers that encompass us and our country ought to make English men and women of this generation glad to be here at such a time. We ought to rejoice at the responsibilities with which destiny has honoured us, and be proud that we are the guardians of our country in an age when her life is at stake.

Winston Churchill
24th April 1943

England That Shall Be

    FOR all of England that is fair
    Is what our dear Lord planted there;
    And all of England that is ill
    Is where we've forced our pagan will;
    And all of England that shall be
    Grows fine or false in men like me.

Lt.-Com. Frederick B. Watt

ALL this I bear, for, what I seek, I know:
Peace, peace is what I seek, and public calm:
Endless extinction of unhappy hates.

Matthew Arnold

The Pessimist

NOTHING to do but work,
Nothing to eat but food,
Nothing to wear but clothes
To keep one from going nude.

Nothing to breathe but air,
Quick as a flash 'tis gone;
Nowhere to fall but off,
Nowhere to stand but on!

B. J. King

Now, my men, every one of you must so act
as to feel that his own will be the chief
contribution to victory. Xenophon

THERE is one thing that is stronger than armies:
an idea whose time is come. Victor Hugo

LIBERTY does not fail those who are determined
to have it. Guiseppe Garibaldi

FAITH means we are convinced of what we do
not see. Hebrews xi. 1 (Moffatt)

If by unworthiness or injustice we debase our
children's conception of parenthood, then by so
doing we debase their conception of God.

MORAL RESPONSIBILITIES

A MAN who is good enough to shed his blood for the country is good enough to be given a square deal afterwards. More than that no man is entitled to, and less than that no man shall have.

Theodore Roosevelt, 1903

THE stern hand of fate has scourged us to an elevation where we can see the great everlasting things that matter for a nation; the great peaks of honour we had forgotten—duty and patriotism clad in glittering white; the great pinnacle of sacrifice pointing like a rugged finger to Heaven.

David Lloyd George
Speech, Queen's Hall, London
19th September 1914

MEANWHILE, if these hours be dark at least do not let us sit deedless, like fools and fine gentlemen, thinking the common toil not good enough for us and beaten by the muddle; but rather let us work like good fellows trying by some dim candle-light to set our workshop ready against tomorrow's light.

William Morris

As a result of long and unbroken Christian usage, it became native to the English to live and work in a society in which moral responsibilities existed. . . . Without justice and charity there can be no England. That is the historic and eternal English vision.

Arthur Bryant

Divine Resources

THERE were evidences that pointed to divine intervention which those in high command came to recognize, and through which they felt that they were watching part of God's plan of the ages working out.

Air-Marshal Sir L. Gossage—
on the Battle of Britain

Horizons

AT once I can tell when a man or a boy has a sense of horizons in his heart. In his eyes his heart implants a wonder, a wistfulness, a serenity, and suggests a 'light that never was on sea or land'. There's a distinction about him; he mixes with us, but you feel that his soul's citizenship is bigger than our little affairs

> ... as some venturer, from his stars receiving
> Promise and presage of sublime emprise,
> Wears evermore the seal of his believing
> Deep in the dark of solitary eyes.

Without horizons what can life be but a mere imprisonment within the walls of so many years?

Sydney Walton

HERE and here did England help me : how can
I help England?—say,
Whoso turns as I, this evening, turn to God to
praise and pray,
While Jove's planet rises yonder, silent over
Africa.

Robert Browning

39

OUR England is a garden, and such gardens are
    not made
By singing : 'Oh, how beautiful!' and sitting
    in the shade,
While better men than we go out and start
    their working lives
At grubbing weeds from gravel-paths with
    broken dinner-knives.

There's not a pair of legs so thin, there's not a
    head so thick,
There's not a hand so weak and white, nor yet
    a heart so sick,
But it can find some needful job that's crying to
    be done,
For the Glory of the Garden glorifieth every one.

Then seek your job with thankfulness and work
    till further orders,
If it's only netting strawberries or killing slugs
    on borders ;
And when your back stops aching and your
    hands begin to harden,
You will find yourself a partner in the Glory of
    the Garden.

Oh, Adam was a gardener, and God who made
    him sees
That half a proper gardener's work is done
    upon his knees ;
So when your work is finished, you can wash
    your hands and pray
For the Glory of the Garden, that it may not
    pass away !
And the Glory of the Garden it shall never pass
    away !   Rudyard Kipling

VI

The Man for the Job

IONA, SCOTLAND
The ancient abbey is being restored

E. W. Tattersall

He builded better than he knew;—
The conscious stone to beauty grew.

VI

The Man for the Job

IN all the business of world-planning, the man is more important than the material. There are ample natural resources to build the houses, but only men and women at their best can make the homes. There is plenty of foodstuff to feed all the world, but only right-minded people can ensure its proper distribution. There is nothing to prevent men living at peace with one another, raising the standard of living and increasing human happiness—nothing except the selfishness of man. The unselfish man is the man for the job!

If, then, we desire this better world we must set out to eliminate human selfishness—but how? I shall not soon forget a conversation with General Sir Bernard Paget, Commander-in-Chief, M.E.F., in which he said, 'There are two main factors in shaping the future life of the world, religion and education'. We agreed that they should be inseparable and in that order.

When you come home, a little dazed by your sudden change in circumstance, and perhaps a little disappointed because you find a world in what seems to be disorderly transition, you ask yourself, 'But what use am I, in such a maelstrom?' The selfish cynic who sets himself the easy task of destructive criticism is no use at all. He is like the spectator at the touch-line who jibes a hard-pressed team making a desperate effort to score. The thing every man has to remember is that he is neither the ball to be kicked this way and that, nor the mere looker-on refusing responsibility. He is in the team! How can he earn his place?—By realizing his personality and relating it to people, to purpose, and to God. This is where religion and education come in—not as auxiliaries, but as essentials.

Your personality is your first asset. Things are not conscious of themselves but persons are. According to Professor Rufus Jones, the marks of personality are (1) power to forecast an end or purpose and to direct action toward it; (2) ability to remember past experiences and to make these memories determine present action; and (3) the power of selecting that which is of *worth*. It is the right use of these tremendous powers which is our responsibility. Personality does not remain static. In our struggle to be worth our place in the team we shall discover that ' every victory confers power for further victory '.

There are two types of people—the one lives ' for the lust of the minute . . . flesh without mind ', the other ' nails all flesh to the Cross till Self dies out in the love of his kind.' These phrases of Tennyson bring us to the problem of self-sacrifice. Self-assertion, at its best, means self-surrender or self-sacrifice. Self-surrender is, in the ultimate, self-affirmation—we surrender the isolated self and realize the true self. This is the Christian view which claims that true freedom is freedom *to bind oneself* to the highest we know. The man for the job is the man who affirms himself by putting the team first. He knows just how long to hold the ball, how to draw the defence, and when to pass or shoot.

It is easy enough to philosophize about all this, but difficult to put it into practice in a world where selfishness still abounds. When the guns ceased to fire in Europe, black markets continued. The whole task is beyond the power of unaided man. There are three things which religion offers: the Book which is the revelation of God to man; prayer which is a means of communication between God and man; and the key to the inexhaustible resources of divine Love in Christ Jesus.

Of the Book, Lord Sankey recently said: ' The desperate condition of Europe demands more than any scheme which political wisdom can devise. We need a reformation which will place the New Order on a Bible basis. To build otherwise is to build on sand.' So

43

much for the wider issue, but of the individual's need Field-Marshal Lord Wolsley said, 'In my humble opinion the soldier who carries the Bible in his pocket possesses what is of far higher value to him than the proverbial Field-Marshal's baton; for if he carries its teaching in his head and lets it rule his heart and conduct, he will certainly be happy and most probably eminently successful'. I have heard that sentiment expressed by many leaders beloved by their men in two great wars. They read their Bibles every day, and their conduct was shaped by its precepts and promises.

But it is not sufficient to read a passage as though it were some magic incantation. The man who is anxious to understand the meaning of the divine purpose for him and for his fellows must read prayerfully. Prayer is the means of communication between man and his Maker. Through prayer he makes contact with God and discovers something of the vastness of the resources at his disposal. Here is part of an ancient prayer, called St. Patrick's Breastplate; if you read these lines thoughtfully, you will see in how many ways a man may look to God for aid.

> I bind unto myself today
> The power of God to hold and lead,
> His eye to watch, His might to stay,
> His ear to hearken to my need,

The wisdom of my God to teach,
   His hand to guide, His shield to ward,
The word of God to give me speech,
   His heavenly host to be my guard.

Christ be with me, Christ within me,
   Christ behind me, Christ before me,
Christ beside me, Christ to win me,
   Christ to comfort and restore me,
Christ beneath me, Christ above me,
   Christ in quiet, Christ in danger,
Christ in hearts of all that love me,
   Christ in mouth of friend and stranger.

In these and countless other ways the Son of Man comes near to help us, but we can so easily remain indifferent to the aid we so desperately need. That prayer of the fifth century is one we might well make our own.

Religion, then, is one of the factors and education the other. 'We need', says General Paget, 'that kind of education which will ensure that we do not lose faith in ourselves and our destiny, as we did after the last war. . . . Moreover, our future will depend far more than it has done in the past upon the character and education of the man in the street, a high proportion of whom are now in the army.'

The man for the job is the man who dares to count himself 'a fellow-labourer with God' and offers himself, body, mind, and spirit to be used by God in the service of his fellows. He will think hard, work hard, and pray hard and, forgetting himself, realize himself. You've been doing that often, 'out yonder'. That's why we welcome you home. *You* are just the man for the job.

FAITH

IT is a plain fact that unless a country bases its life on religious faith it cannot endure.

Field-Marshal Viscount Gort

I FIND that every step in my plan has been taken with the Divine help, and I ask daily for aid, not merely in making the plan, but in carrying it out, and this I hope I shall continue to do until the end of all things which concern me on earth.

Field-Marshal Earl Haig

WHAT is the cause of the lamentable uncertainty which exists today about the deeper things in life? It is surely due to the fact that we have been trying to build upon insecure foundations. The Bible, which reveals God's mind, must once again take its rightful place in our lives and in the life of our nation, and on it we must base our beliefs. The authority of God's Word is the only valid authority by which a sure foundation can be laid for rebuilding our country.

Lieut.-Gen. Sir William G. S. Dobbie

PERSONALITY

SCIENCE may prove the insignificance of this globe in the scale of creation, but it cannot prove the insignificance of man.

Benjamin Disraeli

THE practical power of the English rests on their sincerity. Alfred, whom the affection of the nation makes the type of their race, is called by a writer at the Norman Conquest the Truth-speaker. The phrase of the lowest of the people is *Honour-bright,* and their praise, *His word is as good as his Bond.*

Ralph Waldo Emerson

HARD pounding this, gentlemen; let's see who will pound longest.

Wellington at Waterloo

Lincoln

THE strength of virgin forests braced his mind,
The hush of spacious prairies stilled his soul.
Up from log cabin to the Capitol,
One fire was in his spirit, one resolve—
To send the keen axe to the root of wrong,
Clearing a free way for the feet of God.
And evermore he burned to do his deed
With the fine stroke and gesture of a king:
He built the rail-pile as he built the State,
Pouring his splendid strength thro' every blow.
The conscience of him testing every stroke,
To make his deed the measure of a man.
So came the Captain with the thinking heart.

Edwin Markham

NAPOLEON said: 'An extraordinary power of
influencing and commanding men has been
given to Alexander, Charlemagne, and myself.
But with us the presence has been necessary, the
eye, the voice, the hand. Whereas Jesus Christ
has influenced and commanded His subjects
without His visible bodily presence for eighteen
hundred years!'

Rev. F. Kilvert's Diary

> I have learned
> To look on nature, not as in the hour
> Of thoughtless youth; but hearing often-times
> The still, sad music of humanity,
> Nor harsh, nor grating, though of ample
>   power
> To chasten and subdue. And I have felt
> A presence that disturbs me with the joy
> Of elevated thoughts; a sense sublime
> Of something far more deeply interfused,
> Whose dwelling is the light of setting suns,
> And the round ocean and the living air,
> And the blue sky, and in the mind of man.

William Wordsworth

THERE are four words of salvation for this
country and the whole world—and they are
Faith, Hope, Love, Work.

No Government in this country that has not
faith in the people, hope in the future, love of
its fellow men, and that will not work and work
and work, will bring this country into
better days.

Earl Baldwin

VII

Now Thank we all our God

A   LITTLE   SERVICE

OF

THANKSGIVING

FOR USE IN THE HOME

WILLITON, SOMERSET

H. Smith

Praise God from whom all blessings flow

Now Thank we all Our God

IT's grand to think you're coming back and that your loved ones will see you again, face to face. No one begrudges you a royal welcome. You have earned it, but the best of welcomes means more than hanging out the flags and crossing the threshold of home to be the centre of a happy family festival.

You've often said, 'If I get through this, I'll thank God on my bended knees'. Well, you're through it, and this *is* the moment to thank God. That is why, in this little book of Welcome, we have written a short *Service of Thanksgiving*. Will you read it together? It's the right way to start the next part of life's great adventure.

You have been delivered from the perils of war. You have been delivered to the tasks of peace. This is the moment to dedicate yourself and your loved ones to the service of God and your fellow men. So a house may become a home, and a home become a temple. This is a day of new beginning.

A LITTLE SERVICE
OF
THANKSGIVING

FOR USE IN THE HOME

Scripture Readings

Jesus said : '*Where two or three are gathered together in My name, there am I in the midst of them.*'

St. Matthew xviii. 20

IF it had not been the Lord who was on our side, now may Israel say :

If it had not been the Lord who was on our side, when men rose up against us :

Then had they swallowed us up quick, when their wrath was kindled against us :

Then the waters had overwhelmed us, the stream had gone over our soul :

Then the proud waters had gone over our soul :

Blessed be the Lord, who hath not given us as a prey to their teeth.

Our soul is escaped as a bird out of the snare of the fowlers : the snare is broken and we are escaped.

Our help is in the name of the Lord, who made heaven and earth.

Psalm cxxiv

Jesus said : '*As the Father hath loved Me, so have I loved you : continue ye in My love.*'

St. John xv. 9

LOVE suffereth long and is kind; love envieth not; love vaunteth not itself, is not puffed up.

Doth not behave itself unseemly, seeketh not her own, is not easily provoked, thinketh no evil.

Rejoiceth not in iniquity, but rejoiceth in the truth.

Beareth all things, believeth all things, hopeth all things, endureth all things.

Love never faileth. . . .

1 Corinthians xiii. 4-8

A Prayer of Thanksgiving

(To be said together)

LORD, we come now to Thee to offer thanks for Thy great love which has been about us during the long days of separation. Now Thou hast granted us this crowning mercy. Our hearts are full as we bow ourselves before Thee, here, in this quiet place. Forgive us if we have been impatient and if our faith has faltered. Thou knowest the loneliness and the fears that did beset us. Thou hast brought us through fire and water in safety to this hour. We give Thee our humble thanks, and pray Thy blessing upon our home and our loved ones. May we, mindful of Thy great mercies toward us, be strengthened by Thy grace to do Thy will with joy and in all faithfulness, through Jesus Christ our Lord. *Amen.*

An Act of Dedication

AND now, O Lord, we are no longer our own. We are bought with a price. Take us and make us Thy servants, fearless, obedient, and eager to be used by Thee in the saving of the world. Take our love; our Lord we pour at Thy feet its treasure-store. Take ourselves, and we will be ever, only, all for Thee. *Amen.*

An Act of Remembrance

WE remember, Heavenly Father, those who fell on the field of battle or died on active service, our comrades and our friends. We give thanks for their sacrifice and we trust them to Thy tender mercy, who died to deliver the world from great evil. Comfort those who are left lonely, and grant that we, being spared such great sorrow, may be the more ready to minister to their necessity. Be with our comrades who keep watch and ward on sea and land and in the air. Deliver them, even as Thou hast delivered us. Look, we pray Thee, in pity, upon all mankind so that Thy purposes may be made manifest to all peoples and Thy will be done on earth even as it is done in heaven. Hear us in these our prayers and abide with us, for the sake of Jesus Christ our Lord. *Amen.*

INTO Thy hands we commit ourselves and our loved ones, now and for evermore.

The grace of our Lord Jesus Christ, the love of God and the fellowship of the Holy Spirit be with us now and always. *Amen.*

GOD'S GIFT OF LOVE

In His treatment of children and of His own mother, and in the new meaning which He imparted to the Fatherhood of God, Christ gave to the world a new, a holy ideal of parenthood and, through parenthood, of the sanctity of the home.

J. S. Hoyland

And he who gives a child a home
Builds palaces in Kingdom come. . . .

John Masefield

How do I love thee? Let me count the ways.
I love thee to the depth and breadth and height
My soul can reach, when feeling out of sight
For the ends of Being and ideal Grace.
I love thee to the level of every day's
Most quiet need, by sun and candle light.
I love thee freely, as men strive for Right;
I love thee purely, as they turn from Praise.
I love thee with the passion put to use
In my old griefs, and with my childhood's faith.
I love thee with a love I seemed to lose
With my lost saints—I love thee with the
    breath,
Smiles, tears, of all my life!—and, if God
    choose,
I shall but love thee better after death.

E. B. Browning

PRAYER

Doxologies spring out of devastations and deliverances. . . .

Sydney Walton

Let us thank God in all humility that our nation, our Allies, and our cause so found favour with Him that by His guidance we were enabled to win the battle. May we then ask Him with all trust, so to sustain us that we may be able to continue our present tasks and to perform those that He still requires us to carry out.

Air-Marshal Sir L. Gossage
after the Battle of Britain

Do not say I must wait till this tumult has subsided and I am calm. The worst storm of spirit is the time for prayer : the Agony was the hour of petition.

F. W. Robertson

When God has told you what you ought to do, He has already told you what you can.

Walter Savage Landor

Prayer is the lifting up of the heart to God ; whenever therefore thou attemptest to pray, see that it be thy one design to commune with God, to lift up thy heart to Him, to pour out thy soul before Him.

John Wesley

EVERYDAY PRAYERS

Morning

O LORD, who hast brought us safely through the hours of darkness, lighten our minds that we may greet this new day with reverent joy. It is Thy gift; teach us how best to use its passing hours. Let Thy peace be our strength and our song. We commit ourselves to Thy care; let Thy grace be sufficient for us. Grant us strength for all the duties of the day, and help us so to discharge them that at nightfall we shall have no cause to be ashamed. Hear us for Christ our Saviour's sake. *Amen.*

Evening

Take us, we pray Thee, O Lord of our life, into Thy keeping this night and for ever. O Thou Light of lights, keep us from inward darkness; grant us so to sleep in peace, that we may arise to work according to Thy will, through Jesus Christ our Lord. *Amen.*

For the Peace of God

Grant to us, Lord, the peace which the world cannot give, neither take away. Deliver us from the peril of outward storm and the dominion of inward fear, that we may finish our course and keep the faith, for the sake of Jesus Christ our Saviour. *Amen.*

For the Presence of Jesus

LORD Jesus, who didst come to dwell amongst men and didst share their common life, come again to our poor hearts, that we, compassed about with many cares, may yet feel Thee intimately near through all the hours of this day. Hear our prayer and answer with Thy love. *Amen.*

A Sailor's Prayer

O LORD God, when Thou givest to Thy servants to endeavour any great matter, grant us also to know that it is not the beginning but the continuing of the same, until it be thoroughly finished, which yieldeth the true glory.

Sir Francis Drake

A Soldier's Prayer

ARM me, O thou God of battles, with courage this day, that I may not fall before my enemies. The quarrel is Thine, let the victory be Thine. Tie to my sinews the strength of David that I may with a pebble-stone strike to the earth these giants that fight against Thy Truth. . . . So let me fight that, whether I come off lame or sound, dead or alive, I may live or die Thy soldier. Amen.

Thomas Dekker

VIII

And now we will Build—
Together

MANORBIER CASTLE, SOUTH WALES   *J. A. Brimble*

A man's house is his castle

VIII

And now we Will Build— Together

So we come to the end of this little book. There was so much we wanted to say, but it is sometimes harder to say 'Thank you' than to say 'Please'.

The shouting soon dies down; the flags are taken away. Life stretches before you with its insistent challenge. There are still inequalities and injustices in the world. You were a crusader yesterday, you will be a crusader tomorrow. Perhaps you will find it harder to build up than to destroy, but you have helped to bring mankind to a time of new beginning. That which is to be built must be of beauty, truth, and goodness—a thing to endure, being built upon eternal foundations. Never in our lifetime was there so great an opportunity. We will build a new world after the pattern of God.

'How is it that any great thing is accomplished? By love of justice, by constant devotion to a great cause, and by an unfaltering faith that what is right will in the end succeed.' That was John Bright's belief and it must be ours as we begin again to build.

Two Prime Ministers Look Back

WHEN I look back on the perils which have been overcome, upon the great mountain waves through which the gallant ship has driven, when I remember all that has gone wrong, and remember all that has gone right, I feel sure we have no need to fear the tempest. Let it roar and let it rage. We shall come through.

Winston Churchill

THE world was never conquered by intrigue; it was conquered by faith.

Benjamin Disraeli

A Chinese Blue-print

IF you're planning for one year, plant grain; if you're planning for ten years, plant trees; if you're planning for a hundred years, plant men.

Old Chinese Proverb

Personal Responsibility

EVERY morning and evening, when I say my prayers, I offer up a petition that I shall not be allowed to fail my men.

Field-Marshal Sir Bernard L. Montgomery

WHEN a man assumes a public trust, he should consider himself as public property.

Thomas Jefferson

NOT in the clamour of the crowded street,
Not in the shouts and plaudits of the throng,
But in ourselves, are triumph and defeat.

Longfellow

FOURSCORE and seven years ago our fathers brought forth upon this continent a new nation, conceived in liberty, and dedicated to the proposition that all men are created equal. Now we are engaged in a great civil war, testing whether that nation, or any nation so conceived and so dedicated, can long endure. We are met on a great battlefield of that war. We have come to dedicate a portion of that field as a final resting place for those who here gave their lives that that nation might live. It is altogether fitting and proper that we should do this. But in a larger sense we cannot dedicate, we cannot consecrate, we cannot hallow this ground. The brave men, living and dead, who struggled here, have consecrated it far above our poor power to add or detract. The world will little note, nor long remember, what we say here but it can never forget what they did here. It is for us, the living, rather to be dedicated here to the unfinished work which they who fought here have thus so far nobly advanced. It is rather for us to be dedicated to the great task remaining before us that from these honoured dead we take increased devotion to that cause for which they gave the last full measure of devotion—that we here highly resolve that these dead thall not have died in vain; that this nation, under God, shall have a new birth of freedom, and that government of the people, by the people, for the people, shall not perish from the earth.

The Fight For The Soul

WHAT is threatened today is moral liberty, conscience, respect for the soul, the very nobility of man. To defend the soul, its interests, its rights, its dignity, is the most pressing duty for whoever see the danger. . . . War to all that debases, diminishes, hinders and degrades him; protection for all that fortifies, ennobles, and raises him. The test of every religious, political, or educational system, is the man which it forms. If a system injures the intelligence it is bad. If it injures the character it is vicious. If it injures the conscience it is criminal.

Amiel

MAN has lost his balance, because he has lost his spiritual centre, and lost the one religion *which unifies life*.

Thomas Masaryk

SHALL not England still be in the van, as she has always been? Never yet has she failed in the good cause, and never will she. Has she not ever struck for Freedom and the Cross?— Inseparable watchwords, that the experience of the world has taught us must go hand in hand, or not at all; and where she strikes, good faith, she drives well home.

G. J. Whyte-Melville

THE CITY OF GOD

And I saw a new heaven and a new earth: for the first heaven and the first earth were passed away; and there was no more sea.

And I John saw the holy city, new Jerusalem, coming down from God out of heaven, prepared as a bride adorned for her husband.

And I heard a great voice out of heaven saying, Behold the tabernacle of God is with men, and He will dwell with them, and they shall be His people, and God Himself shall be with them, and be their God.

And God shall wipe away all tears from their eyes. . . .

And the city had no need of the sun, neither of the moon, to shine in it: for the glory of God did lighten it and the Lamb is the light thereof.

And the nations of them which are saved shall walk in the light of it: and the kings of the earth do bring their glory and honour into it. . . .

In the midst of the street of it, and on either side of the river, was there the tree of life, which bore twelve manner of fruits, and yielded her fruit every month: and the leaves of the tree were for the healing of the nations.

And there shall be no more curse: but the throne of God and of the Lamb shall be in it; and His servants shall serve Him:

And they shall see His face. . . .

The Book of Revelation

RING out false pride in place and blood,
   The civic slander and the spite;
   Ring in the love of truth and right,
Ring in the common love of good.

Ring out old shapes of foul disease;
   Ring out the narrowing lust of gold;
   Ring out the thousand wars of old,
Ring in the thousand years of peace.

Ring in the valiant man and free,
   The larger heart, the kindlier hand;
   Ring out the darkness of the land,
Ring in the Christ that is to be.

                                          Tennyson

Evening Prayer

O LORD support us all the day long, till the
shadows lengthen, and the evening comes, and
the busy world is hushed, and the fever of life is
over, and our work is done! Then in Thy
mercy give us a safe lodging, and a holy rest,
and peace at the last.

ACKNOWLEDGEMENTS

GRATEFUL thanks are due to the following for their kind permission to include extracts from copyright works in this booklet. If in any instances such rights have been unwittingly infringed, Dr. Church trusts he may be pardoned and informed of his mistake.

Messrs. George Allen & Unwin, Ltd., and the Author, for a quotation from *Margaret Macdonald* by Ramsay Macdonald.

Messrs. William Collins, Sons & Co., Ltd., and the Author, for an extract from *English Saga* by Arthur Bryant.

Messrs. Macmillan & Co., Ltd., and the Author, for poem 'But to Come Home!' from *Collected Poems 1905-25* by Wilfrid Gibson.

Messrs. Macmillan & Co., Ltd., and the Author's Executors, for quotation from 'For England's Sake' from *Poems* by W. E. Henley.

Messrs. Macmillan & Co., Ltd., and the Trustees of the Hardy Estate for poem 'In Time of "the Breaking of Nations"' from the *Collected Poems of Thomas Hardy*.

Messrs. Faber & Faber, Ltd., for verse from 'Another Time' by W. H. Auden.

Messrs. Hodder & Stoughton, Ltd., and the Authors, for extracts from *Margaret Ogilvy* by Sir James Barrie, and from *Old Memories* by Sir Henry Jones.

The Oxford University Press and Mrs. Laurence Binyon for verses by Laurence Binyon.

The Proprietors of 'Punch' for verse from 'Between Midnight and Morning' by Sir Owen Seaman.

The Epworth Press for extracts from *Getting Rid of God* by F. C. Spurr and *Christ and National Reconstruction* by J. S. Hoyland.

The Editor of *The Daily Sketch* for extract from an article by General Dobbie.

Oxford University Press and Mrs. George Bambridge for quotation from 'The Glory of the Garden' from *A School History of England* by Rudyard Kipling.

Dr. Church is also grateful to his friends Sydney Walton, C.B.E., M.A., B. Litt., for quotations from *The Sieve of Blindness* (Epworth Press), Mr. and Mrs. Annakin for 'Springtime in England', lines written by their son, and Prof. T. E. Jessop for a quotation from *Effective Religion* (Epworth Press).

Cover photographs—Chipping Campden by E. W. Tattersall; St. Martin-in-the-Fields by E. F. Cox.

MADE AND PRINTED IN GREAT BRITAIN BY
RUSH & WARWICK (BEDFORD) LTD., BEDFORD